simple machines

Wheels and Cranks

David Glover

RIGBY
INTERACTIVE
LIBRARY

Printed in Hong Kong / China

01 00
10 9 8 7 6 5 4 3

Library of Congress Cataloging-in-Publication Data
Glover, David.
    Wheels and cranks / David Glover.
        p.   cm — (Simple machines)
    Includes index.
    Summary: Introduces the principles of wheels and cranks as simple machines, using examples from everyday life.
    ISBN 1–57572–081–7 (lib. bdg.)
    1. Wheels—Juvenile literature. 2. Cranks and crankshafts—Juvenile literature.
[1. Wheels. 2. Cranks and crankshafts.]
I. Title. II. Series.
TJ181.5.G55 1997
621.8 ' 11—dc20   96–15814
                                                          CIP
                                                           AC

Designed by Celia Floyd and Sharon Rudd
Illustrated by Barry Atkinson (pp. 5, 17, 21); Douglas Hall (p. 6); and Tony Kenyon (p. 4)

Acknowledgments
The publisher would like to thank the following for permission to reproduce photographs:
Trevor Clifford, pp. 5, 6, 7, 19 *top*, 22, 23; Zefa, pp. 8, 9, 11, 15 *bottom*, 18; Tony Stone Worldwide, p. 10; Stockfile/Steven Behr, p. 12; Lori Adamski Peek/TSW, p. 13; TRIP/R Drury, p. 14/G. Horner, p. 20; Quadrant Picture Library, p. 15 *top*; Panos Pictures/Ron Giling, p. 16; Derek Cattani/Zefa, p. 17; Mary Evans Picture Library, p. 19; Collections/Brian Shuel, p. 21.

Cover photograph by Trevor Clifford

Every effort has been made to contact copyright holders of any material reproduced in this book. Any omissions will be rectified in subsequent printings if notice is given to the publisher.

Note to the Reader

Some words in this book are printed in **bold** type. This indicates that the word is listed in the glossary on page 24. This glossary gives a brief explanation of words that may be new to you and tells you the page on which each word first appears.

Contents

What Are Wheels and Cranks?

The wheel is one of the most important **inventions** ever made. Wheels are round, and they turn to make things go. There are wheels on toys, bicycles, trains, cars and trucks.

If no one had invented the wheel, people would have to walk everywhere. We would need to carry things on our backs or drag them along the ground.

crank handle

turn

If a handle is put on one side of a wheel, it can be used to turn the wheel. This handle is called a *crank*. Sometimes a crank handle is just a bent bar.

You turn a crank handle to work this pencil sharpener.

Rollers

This circus performer is learning how to walk on a barrel. The barrel rolls along under her feet.

Workers can use rollers to move heavy loads. The ancient Egyptians built the pyramids by dragging huge stones on rollers. The rollers were made from tree trunks.

You can do the same thing using pencils to move a book. As one pencil is uncovered behind the book as it moves forward, pick it up and move it to the front.

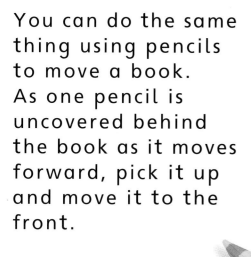

FACT FILE

From rollers to wheels

It is possible that the use of rollers long ago gave people the idea for the first wheels.

Cart and Car Wheels

Wheels like the ones on this old
cart have been made for hundreds
of years. The wheels on this cart
are made from wood. A metal hoop
is fixed around the wheel to stop
it from wearing away. These wheels
give a very bumpy ride.

The wheels on modern cars have thick rubber tires wrapped around them. The tires are filled with air, like balloons. This helps the tires to bounce over bumps on the road.

The pattern that is cut into a tire is called the **tread.** The tread helps the tire **grip** on wet roads.

FACT FILE

Who invented the wheel?

No one knows who invented the wheel. People may have invented wheels in different parts of the world at different times. Carts with wheels were made in ancient Egypt more than 5,000 years ago.

Bicycle Wheels

A racing bicycle has very light wheels. Thin wire **spokes** hold the **rims** of the wheels in place and help them keep their shape. Wheels like these are good for riding fast on smooth roads.

A mountain bike has much thicker wheels than a racing bike. They are heavier and make the bike slower, but they are stronger. Wheels like these are good for riding over rough ground.

Boards and Blades

A skateboard has two pairs of small rubber wheels. Each wheel spins around on a **rod**. This rod is called an **axle**. Inside the wheels are small metal balls called **ball bearings**. They make the wheels turn smoothly.

These roller blades have four hard plastic wheels in a row. The stiff boots help you balance and support your ankles. Even though roller blade wheels are small, expert roller bladers can ride very fast.

FACT FILE

Skating tip

Skateboards and roller blades go best on smooth, hard ground. Their small wheels don't work well on grass.

Tractor and Truck Wheels

Big wheels keep a tractor from sinking in soft mud. The deep tread on the tires gives extra grip when the ground is slippery.

This truck can go almost anywhere on its huge wheels. It can drive through deep water and climb steep hills. It can even drive over other trucks!

FACT FILE

Giant trucks

The biggest tires in the world are twice as tall as an adult. They are fitted to giant dump trucks.

Crank Handles

This machine is used for crushing sugar cane to squeeze out the juice. The mules are turning the crank handle as they walk around. This makes the rollers turn and crush the sugar cane.

There is a crank handle on this old car. You turn the handle to start the engine. Modern cars have a separate starter **motor** that is worked by turning a key.

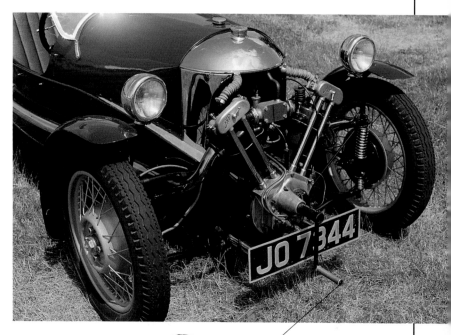

crank handle

FACT FILE

crank handle

crank handle

Records and movies

The first record players and movie cameras had crank handles to make them work. Today, many machines are powered by electric motors.

Pedal Power

This woman turns her spinning wheel by pedaling with her foot. The pedal pushes a crank, which makes the wheel turn.

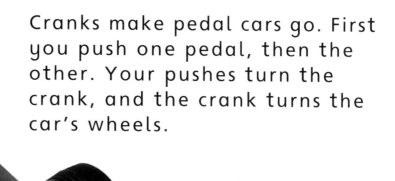

Cranks make pedal cars go. First you push one pedal, then the other. Your pushes turn the crank, and the crank turns the car's wheels.

FACT FILE

Cycles and cranks

The very first bicycles were worked by cranks, just as they are today. The cyclist pushed the pedals down one at a time to make the wheels turn.

More Cranks

A lock is a canal with gates at each end. It is used to raise and lower boats from one level of water to another. A crank handle opens one lock gate at a time to let the water through.

An **organ grinder** turns a crank handle to make music. The organ plays tunes as he winds the handle. The quicker the handle is turned, the faster the music plays.

FACT FILE

Winding up

The handle on a well is a crank. It winds up the rope to lift the bucket.

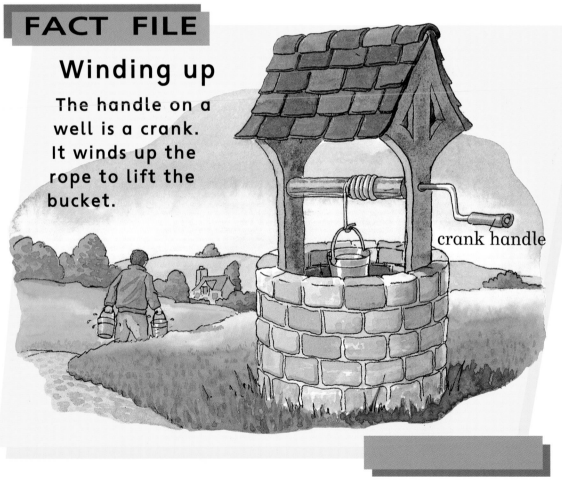

crank handle

Crank Toys

This garden windmill works when the wind blows. The wind makes the windmill turn. The windmill turns a crank, which makes the man wind up the bucket from the well.

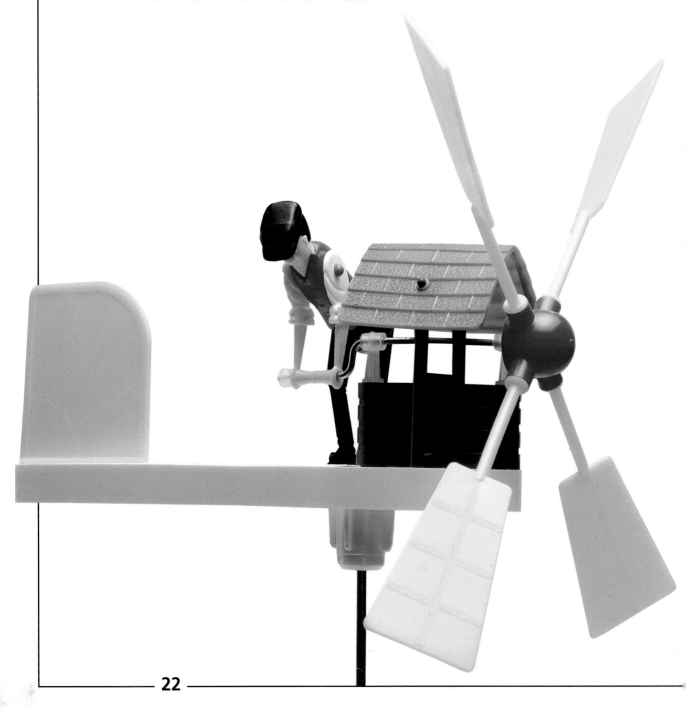

A crank turns the wheel on this model steam engine. The steam pushes a rod inside a tube. This rod is called a **piston**. The piston pushes the crank and the wheel turns around.

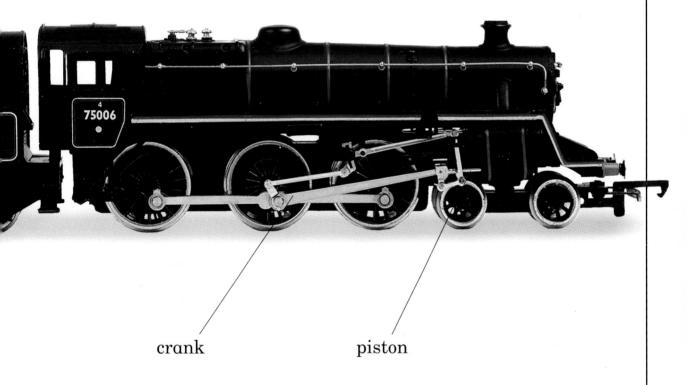

crank   piston

FACT FILE

Batteries not included

Early versions of toys with moving parts used cranks. Today, most moving toys are battery operated.

Glossary

axle Rod or bar that runs from the center of one wheel to the center of another **12**

ball bearings Metal balls inside a wheel which make it turn smoothly **12**

grip To hold tightly **9**

inventions New machines that no one has made before **4**

motor Machine that uses electricity or fuel to make things move **17**

organ grinder Street musician who plays an organ by turning its handle **21**

piston Rod inside a tube that is pushed by steam to make a crank turn **23**

rims Outside edge of a wheel **10**

rod Bar or stick, often made from metal **12**

saddle sore Feeling uncomfortable after sitting on a hard seat for too long **11**

spokes Metal wires that hold the rim of a bicycle wheel in place and help keep its shape **10**

tread Pattern in a rubber tire that helps it grip the road when it is wet or muddy **9**

Index

Further Readings

Barton, Byron. *Machines at Work*. New York: HarperCollins, 1987.

Graham, Ian. *Cars, Bikes, Trains & Other Land Machines*. New York: Kingfisher, 1993.

Lampton, Christopher. *Marbles, Roller Skates, Doorknobs: Simple Machines That are Really Wheels*. Brookfield, CT: Millbrook Press, 1991.